Word Bird's Magic Wand

Published in the United States of America by The Child's World®, Inc.
PO Box 326
Chanhassen, MN 55317-0326
800-599-READ
www.childsworld.com

Project Manager Mary Berendes
Editor Katherine Stevenson, Ph.D.
Designer Ian Butterworth

Library of Congress Cataloging-in-Publication Data
Moncure, Jane Belk.
Word Bird's magic wand / by Jane Belk Moncure.
p. cm.
Summary: Word Bird uses a pencil as a magic wand
to write and learn new words.
ISBN 1-56766-630-2 (lib. : alk. paper)
[1. Vocabulary—Fiction. 2. Pencils—Fiction. 3. Birds—Fiction.]
I. Title.
PZ7.M739 Wog 2002
[E]—dc1F
2001006055

Word Bird's

Magic Wand

by Jane Belk Moncure

illustrated by Chris McEwan

Happy Birthday! Love, Word Bird

"Today is my mama's birthday,"
said Word Bird. "I will paint a
picture for her."

When the paint was dry, Word Bird
wrote some words with a pencil.
"My pencil is a magic wand. Look
what it can do," Word Bird said.

"My pencil is a magic wand, too,"
said Bee. "I can write words with it,
just as you can. My card is for my
friend. My friend is sick."

Kk Ll Mm Nn Oo Pp Qq Rr Ss Tt Uu Vv Ww Xx Yy Zz

soon!

"I like your pictures and your words,"
said their teacher, Miss Beary.

"I want to write words," said Frog.
"Me too," said Duck.
"Have a magic wand,"
   said Word Bird.

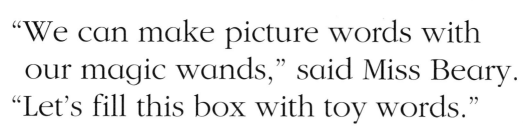

"We can make picture words with
our magic wands," said Miss Beary.
"Let's fill this box with toy words."

Frog made a robot.
Duck made a truck.

What did Word Bird make?

The next day, Word Bird and Frog
made number words.

Miss Beary made word banks for them.
"You can put your number words in
your word banks," she said.

Every day, Word Bird wrote words
with the magic wand. Word Bird
wrote words on signs for a zoo.

Word Bird helped make signs
for Cat's airport.
"Thanks, Word Bird," said Cat.

15

Others made signs, too. Pig used a
magic wand to make a lunch sign.
"Yum, yum!" said Word Bird.

News Flash!
Get your
umbrella.
Rain today.

Dog made a news sign with a
magic wand. Cat did not like
the news—but Duck did!

Word Bird says, "Do a flip."

One rainy spring day, Miss Beary said, "Tell me about funny things you like to do." Then she made signs with her magic wand.

Word Bird and Duck helped her
put the signs all around the room.

19

"Read the signs. Do what they say,"
said Miss Beary.

Frog says, "Jump."

Cat says, "Tiptoe."

Bee says, "Crawl."

Word Bird giggled. "What a wacky walk," Word Bird said.

Another day, Word Bird wrote a secret note with a magic wand. Where did Word Bird hide the note? In the lunch box!

Word Bird gave the note to Duck
at lunchtime. Duck was surprised!

Word Bird wrote with a magic wand
all year. One day, Word Bird cut out
a big paper circle. Word Bird wrote
words around and around the circle.

The most exciting day of my life was the day I went to the zoo.

ZOO

Word Bird gave the circle to Duck. "Turn it around and around," Word Bird said. "You can read it. It's my circle story."

My
Dinosaur Book
by Word Bird

Then Word Bird wrote a whole book.
Can you guess what it was about?

Word Bird read the book to the class.
Everyone clapped.
"I can write a book, too," said Mouse.

Mouse held up the new book.
"Guess who lives in my house?"
Mouse asked.
"Who?" asked Word Bird.
"Read my book to find out," said
Mouse. Word Bird read about
Mouse and Mouse's family.

Bee made an ABC book.
"'A' is for apple. 'B' is for you,
Word Bird," Bee said.
"Wow!" said Word Bird.
"That's neat."

"I have a surprise for you," said Miss
  Beary. She gave buttons to Word
  Bird and all the other friends.
"What do the buttons say?" she asked.
"I am an author," said Word Bird.

You can be an author, too. You can
write a book with your magic wand!

Can you write these words with Word Bird?

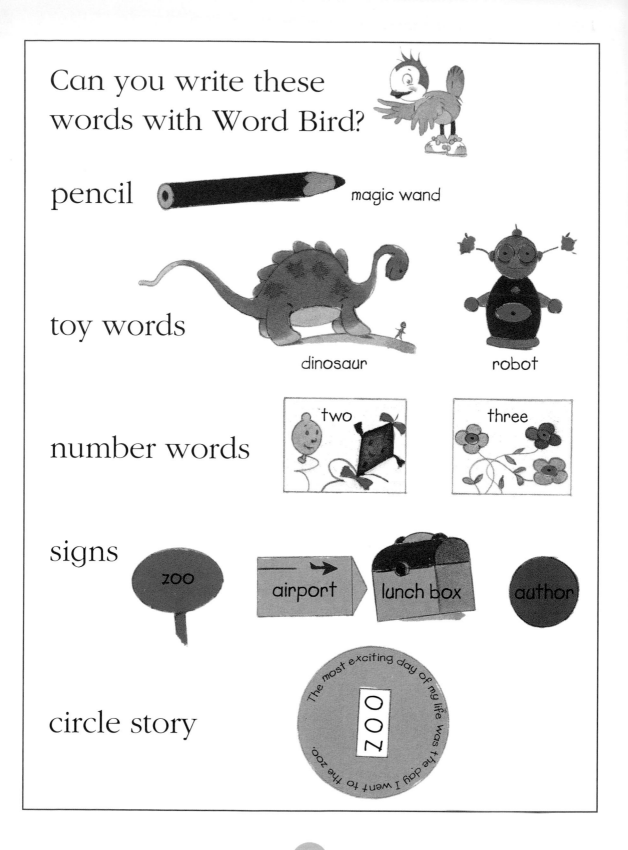

pencil

magic wand

toy words

dinosaur

robot

number words

two

three

signs

zoo

airport

lunch box

author

circle story

The most exciting day of my life was the day I went to the zoo.

zoo